My First Chinese Picture Books for Short Sentences Book 1

我的第一套中文短句绘本 1

Xiaolin Huang

To Cooper and Danna for being the pilot readers

First Published in Australia in 2017
This edition published in 2017
by Xiaolin Huang
ABN 60 520 297 573

127 Cambridge Cres
Wyndham Vale
VIC 3024, Australia

http://fb.me/mfcpb

National Library of Australia Cataloguing-in-Publication entry

Creator: Huang, Xiaolin, author.

Title: My first Chinese picture books for short sentences. Book 1
: 我的第一套中文短句绘本 第一册 / Xiaolin Huang.

ISBN: 9780648102502 (paperback)

Target Audience: For preschool age

Subjects: Chinese characters--Juvenile literature
Chinese language--Writing--Juvenile literature
Chinese language--Juvenile literature
Picture books for children

我的床

我的书

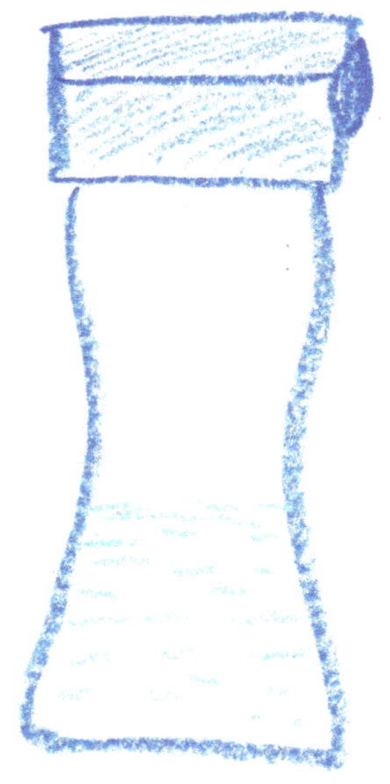

我的杯子

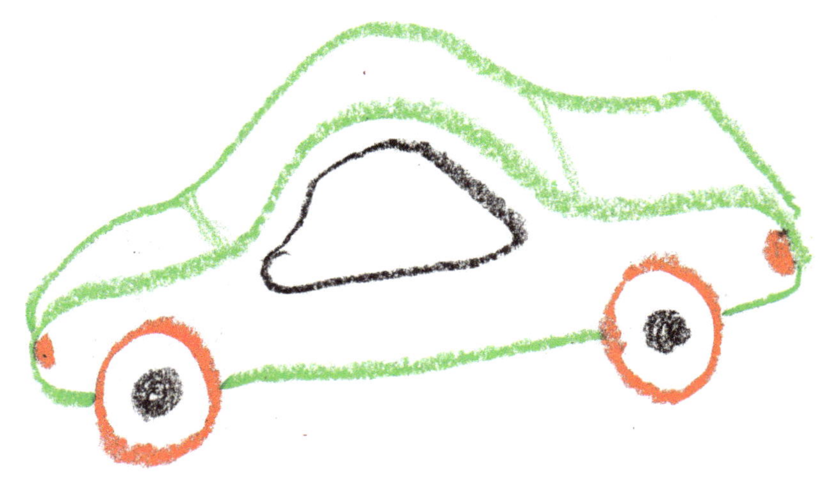

我的车子

我的钢琴

我的家

妈妈的梳子

爸爸的电脑

山上有树

山上有灯塔

天上有太阳

天上有月亮

天上有白云

天上有小鸟

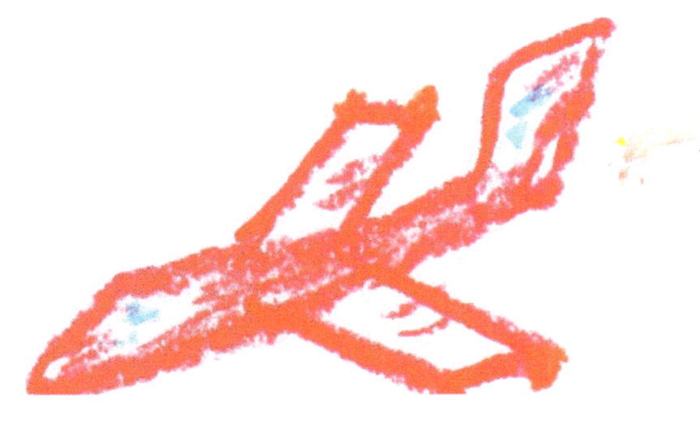

天上有飞机

水里有螃蟹

水里有小鱼

树上有小鸟

地上有小花

完

The End

本书常见字 试着写一写认一认

Frequently Used Characters
Try to write and recognise them

子	山	上
天	小	太
门	飞	白
云	我	的
有	鸟	书

www.ingramcontent.com/pod-product-compliance
Lightning Source LLC
Chambersburg PA
CBHW041211100726
47911CB00017B/920

* 9 7 8 0 6 4 8 1 0 2 5 0 2 *